When Apples Ain't Enough

When Apples Ain't Enough

Career Change Techniques for Teachers, Counselors and Librarians

Jean M. Miller
and
Georgianna M. Dickinson

Jalmar Press • Sacramento, California

Jalmar Press, Inc.
6501 Elvas Avenue
Sacramento, California 95819
(916) 451-2897

Dedicated to Gary in
appreciation of his support.

ACKNOWLEDGMENTS

We, the co-authors, wish to acknowledge the following people for their contributions to this book.

We wish to thank Walter Scott, Jr., for his moral support and encouragement.

We wish to thank Ranny Riley, President of Career Design, 2398 Broadway, San Francisco, California 94115, for her permission to use the list of "Function Words to Describe Skills" in Appendix A and the "Examples of Areas of Effectiveness" in Appendix B. Career Design is a management consulting company which designs and implements career development systems in corporations, and offers seminars and counseling to men and women in career transition.

We wish to express gratitude and thanks to Clare Reich for her constructive ideas and to Barbara McConnell for the list of counseling duties.

TABLE OF CONTENTS

Whatever you can do,
or dream you can,
begin it.
Boldness has
genius, power and magic
in it.   Goethe

INTRODUCTION

We, the authors of this book, are two educators, Georgianna M. Dickinson, B.A. in American Culture (Mount Holyoke College, South Hadley, Massachusetts), M.S. in Education: Counseling and Guidance (Cornell University, Ithaca, New York), and Jean M. Miller, B.S. in Education (University of Wisconsin, River Falls, Wisconsin), M.A. in Library Science (Rosary College, River Forest, Illinois). Both of us have been "insiders" who carefully considered various "outside" alternatives to education. While in the process of changing careers, we learned many things which we decided would be helpful to other teachers, counselors and librarians. We did extensive research on the topic of job searching, participated in job search seminars and workshops and attended career counseling sessions. From these experiences, we learned that it is extremely difficult to transfer job skills from education to the business world where there are different terms, goals and values. Since none of the seminars, books, workshops, and counseling sessions was specifically designed for the educator, we planned this book for fellow teachers, counselors and librarians who find themselves facing an unknown job market in a world which is foreign to them and for which they may feel totally unprepared.

In discussing job dissatisfactions with other educators, their complaints and concerns centered around such stressful sociological conditions as: discipline problems, violence, physical exhaustion, lack of administrative support, lack of appreciation, overcrowded classes, and lack of administrative concern for the individual needs of both teachers and students. Dismay and alarm were also expressed over other realistic situations such as declining enrollment, adverse legislation, massive layoffs, financial cut-backs, and the fact that educational standards are being geared to the lowest possible denominator.

Thus, this book could be entitled a "survival kit" as its purpose is to help fellow teachers, counselors and librarians make the transition from the education to the business world. If you are ready for a career change, it is necessary to weigh the advantages and disadvantages of each of these worlds.

Before you decide to change careers rather than remain and face the problems inherent in the structure of today's school system, ask yourself whether or not your reasons for leaving education are valid. Consider that the business world is harsh, demanding and competitive. Do you want to function in this type of environment? Weigh the relative pros and cons of a large company structure and organization against your smaller system. You will be faced with a different frame of reference in the business world where the values and priorities are based on money, where competition is keen and where there is concern for promotion and self-advancement.

You will also be faced with certain unfamiliar realities which at first may appear as cold, hard facts. For example, you may have to consider a cut in salary in your initial change into business. This should be weighed against the favorable possibility that your pay raises may be more frequent with merit raises based on performance ratings. Some companies evaluate you every three months, some every four months, some every six months, etc. You may want to negotiate this before you accept a position.

Other disadvantages to business are obvious facts such as shorter vacations, lack of three-month summer vacations and the absence of tenure or guarantee of permanent employment. In addition, there may or may not be comparable retirement, medical and dental benefits. You may want to take a "leave of absence" from your present position in order to determine whether or not the business world is for you rather than resign and later regret it.

Assuming that you have considered all of the above-listed relative and pertinent advantages and disadvantages of business versus education and that you are now determined to leave the teaching, counseling or librarian profession, this book is designed to help you transfer your job skills into business language and achieve success in finding a job in the business world. The following areas are covered: Determining Values, Identifying and Assessing Marketable Job Skills, Focusing, Networking, Informational Interviewing, Organizing a Resume, Writing a Resume, Writing a Cover Letter, and Interviewing Techniques. Sample resumes for a teacher, a counselor and a librarian, and a sample cover letter are included in the appendix, along with a list of employment resources, sample career objectives for educators and suggested reading materials.

As you begin your creative job search, it is essential to realize that it will take a great deal of time and patience. There are some suggestions that we feel might be beneficial to you. First of all, job hunting can be an exhausting and frustrating experience. Try to keep it in perspective without giving up other values that are important to you. For example, friends, social activities, sports, and recreation can be very important to you during your search.

Secondly, talk over problems, successes and failures with at least one good friend. Try to project self-confidence, enthusiasm and faith in yourself.

Set specific daily goals for yourself, such as placing two job-related telephone calls per day. Finally, face your fear of the unknown. Go out, meet it, and conquer it. Remember that you are taking a big step toward self-realization and assuming responsibility for yourself. Good luck as you begin your career change.

DETERMINING YOUR VALUES

At the beginning of your creative job search, you need to determine what your values are. Before you determine where you are going with your life's work, you must examine your interests and values in order to determine short and long term goals. Think of the things which are of most importance to you and establish a hierarchy of values. In the past, what was important to you in teaching was probably related to the satisfactions you gained from helping others to learn. These satisfactions relate to the values of knowledge, wisdom, work independence, and academic achievement. Now, your priorities and values are probably shifting due to the need to change careers. What are your values now? To help you determine which things are of utmost importance in your life at the present time, there are a few simple exercises you can do.

First, examine your environment. Look at your behavior and

attitudes and try to perceive the way you act toward other people. Ask yourself what you like to do best. Write down a list of the achievements of which you are most proud. After each achievement, write the letter "P" beside it if it involves other people or teamwork, and the letter "A" beside it if it is your own solitary achievement. Next, try to find and list strengths from these achievements which you have recognized as solid accomplishments. Special talents and abilities will emerge which you can include in your resume.

If you wrote a "P" next to most of your achievements, it is an indication that you enjoy working with other people. If you wrote mostly "A's" next to your achievements, it indicates that you prefer to work alone. It is important to realize whether you like to work with people or to work by yourself before embarking upon your career change.

List of Achievements

Next, consider questions such as: Whom and what do I live for?
What is the meaning of life for me now? What does my life mean
to others now? Do I foster creativity in myself and others? What
is really important to me?

After mulling over these questions, write down a list of 20 things
you enjoy doing. After each item, again write a "P" if it involves
other people or teamwork, an "A" if it is an activity you do alone,
and a "$" if it costs more than $3.00. "NC" denotes that it is free
of charge. Then, think about what you have learned about yourself.
Do all your activities involve money or are most of them independent of cost (such as walking on the beach or looking at a sunset)?

List of 20 Items

1.

2.

3.

4.

5.

6.

7.

8.

9.

10.

11.

12.

13.

14.

15.

16.

17.

18.

19.

20.

If most of the 20 things you just listed have a "P" next to them, it indicates that you like to do things with other people. If most of the 20 items you just listed have an "A" next to them, it is an indication that you prefer doing things alone. The number of "$" signs listed is an indication of how much money you will need to earn in order to live in the manner to which you are accustomed.

The previous exercise will help you complete the next one. List the 5 most important things that you value in your life today. What are the things in which you believe? What are the ideals for which you strive? Rate these 5 most important values from 1 to 5, with 1 being the most important and 5 being the least important.

Values

1.

2.

3.

4.

5.

Next, read the following list; select and rate the 5 values which are most important to you. Again, 1 should be the most important rating, with 5 being the least important.

Social gatherings

Material success in chosen profession

Recognition from others in chosen profession

Fame and national recognition for creativity or popularity, such as "teacher of the year"

Sense of humor

Closeness of relationships with family, friends

Independence in job and personal life

Power over peers

Power over students

Academic achievement/educational degrees

Love

Admiration

Praise of others

Loyalty to causes

Loyalty to friends, groups, institutions, professional associations

Services to friends, groups, institutions, professional associations

Peace of mind/contentment

Exercise, body awareness, sports activities

Good health

Attractive appearance through good looks, grooming, clothes

Acquisition of knowledge for sense of self-worth

Strong, undoubting religious faith

Hedonistic delights, such as eating, drinking, sexual pleasure

Leisure to enjoy the pleasure of "being a bum" or "doing nothing all day long"

Common sense

Security of financial independence and retirement planning

Aesthetic awareness and appreciation

Fair and equal treatment for everyone regardless of race or background

Social consciousness to fight to eliminate poverty and disease

Wisdom

Judgment

Empathy for others

Insight and intuition

Integrity, honesty

Creative innovations

Sensitivity to others' needs and wants

In interpreting your answers, try to figure out if you would be happier working with people or working alone. Are you more comfortable with facts, figures and machines than with people? Are you independent of outside direction and leadership? If you value a sense of humor and are supportive of people, you might consider a position in human resources. If you are a creative type who prefers to design or experiment, consider a position where you can work independently in an office or in a laboratory. If you have placed loyalty to friends, groups, institutions, or professional associations at the top of your list, you may wish to relate this to a public relations position. If you place a high value on financial rewards for work well done, you might want to consider a position in sales where your financial gain will be commensurate with the time you spend on the job.

You should have discovered things you did not know about yourself by completing these value judgment exercises. Also, you should now be in a position to define your goals in terms of the things which are most important to you.

After you define your goals, the next step is to identify and assess your marketable job skills. This is the subject of the following chapter.

IDENTIFYING AND ASSESSING
YOUR MARKETABLE JOB SKILLS

Identifying and assessing your marketable job skills will be the most time-consuming task of all. It is absolutely essential to think about how you see yourself. Then, think about these skills and determine where they might be useful.

In making a career change outside the field of education, there are four options to consider.

1. The same group of skills can be used in a new setting. Working on a consulting, free-lance basis would be an example of using your same skills in a new setting.

2. One or two skills can be expanded upon in order to find a new career. A job as a researcher, editor or writer would fit into this category.

3. Added training or education can be sought. This is something to consider if you have the necessary time and money.

4. A completely new career can be undertaken. This also takes time and money.

Most of you would probably choose option #1 or option #2 due to the fact that it is too expensive to seek added education or training or to undertake a new career. Therefore, it is essential for you to concentrate on and expand upon those skills that you already have in order to transfer them to the business world.

In identifying and assessing your own job skills, you must first recognize that you are unique. No one else has the talents and strengths that you have. Be positive. Think about all the strong, helpful, resourceful things you do every day. You are a helping person or you would not have chosen education as a profession.

Administrators rarely give any bouquets of gratitude to you for your everyday performance. On the evaluations you have received from administrators, your strengths have probably been minimized or overlooked. Educational evaluations are often designed in a negative manner with little praise for a job well done.

What about your communication and organizational skills? You have them, and business needs them! For each class you face every day, there has to be organization and planning. Lesson plans must be devised, and units must be planned in advance. Of course, you say. I know all this. You know it, but business does not. Business is out of touch with the educational world, and it is up to you to inform the business community what you actually do on your job and how it relates to the skills that are needed for your new job. You are able to give adequate directions so that others may follow your instructions and carry them out. You are able to answer questions. You are able to relate adequately in interpersonal situations. All of these things involve an advanced degree of talent in communication and organization skills.

The second step in your creative job search is to identify, assess and list your job skills in any order you choose. How do you accomplish this? Review briefly the professional duties you perform. As a teacher, you probably use the following important job skills in the classroom:

Communicating

Evaluating performance

Testing performance

Writing instructions

Relating instructions verbally

Communicating clearly what you expect in the way of performance

Writing goals and objectives

Communicating answers to questions

Communicating instructions to staff assistants (teacher aides)

Communicating instructions to student aides

Directing and supervising staff assistants and student aides

Solving human relations problems

Maintaining discipline and order

Creating atmosphere conducive to learning

Encouraging, motivating, generating enthusiasm

Motivating for effective achievement and excellence in performance

Selling yourself as a trustworthy person

Selling yourself as a skilled person in your field

Selling yourself as a worthwhile individual

Demonstrating skills and techniques

Illustrating ideas and varying the instructional program by using audio-visual materials

Outside the classroom, you probably use many of the following self-motivated job skills:

Planning units of instruction for day, week, month

Initiating and developing job training programs for staff assistants and student aides

Solving problems of financial management

Researching and coordinating pilot programs

Communicating successfully with co-workers, counselors, parents, administrators

Interviewing and counseling students

Writing student recommendations for jobs and colleges

Developing and devising methods for course development, changes and improvement

Creating innovations in your specialized subject

Revising and updating teaching materials, plans and techniques

Writing reports

Directing public relations programs using community resources

Developing achievement tests

Budgeting and ordering supplies

Many of the teacher skills also pertain to counselors and librarians. However, there are specific skills unique to these two groups. The following skills are unique to counselors:

Arbitrating and negotiating disputes and misunderstandings between personnel

Interpreting and integrating test results to create personnel profiles

Facilitating communication between personnel at all levels

Facilitating time-management studies

Determining job skills

Evaluating data

Scheduling and programming

Promoting cross-cultural communication

Researching and presenting material on colleges/projects/employment

Conducting and supervising promotional fund-raising activities

Compiling, writing and evaluating reports

Developing, promoting and publicizing public relations programs

Developing, implementing and coordinating career orientation and career counseling sessions using variety of media, methods and speakers

Evaluating personnel and writing recommendations

Projecting and maintaining confidentiality

Librarians use the following important specific job skills unique to their position:

Managing library facility

Budgeting for supplies, books, equipment, and materials

Purchasing supplies, books, equipment, and materials

Supervising and evaluating professional and clerical staff

Instructing personnel in use of audio-visual materials and equipment

Planning, organizing and producing audio-visual materials

Developing and presenting orientation programs

Organizing and training volunteers

Surveying, analyzing and coordinating budget projections for entire institution

Performing needs-assessment studies

Preparing loss-control reports

Researching information

Negotiating with vendors

Always think in terms of strong, simple action verbs. (See "Function Words to Describe Skills" in Appendix A.) For example, "I budgeted and ordered supplies," not, "I was responsible for writing budgets and ordering supplies." Or, "I supervised 40 people," not, "I was in charge of 40 persons."

You must identify and list your job skills and choose those that you wish to transfer to your next job in the business world. Note the skills you have enjoyed most. You are going to want to enjoy that next job!

FOCUSING

Focusing on a particular job will probably be one of the most difficult parts of your creative job search. Since your resume can include only one career objective, it is imperative for you to analyze and categorize your skills, job experience and abilities in order to focus on a particular job.

The focusing process may take hours of energy, time and effort on your part. Ask friends, relatives, associates, and neighbors to talk about their jobs, their aspirations and the procedures they followed when they focused on their careers. Do not hesitate to ask questions of these people which will help you to focus. Focusing can be a frustrating experience; however, remain calm. If you talk with many different people in many different occupations and read extensively on the subject, you are bound to uncover enough information about jobs and job titles in order to focus clearly upon a particular job.

Ask yourself what job would be best suited for you. Sift facts, eliminate some possibilities, consider other possibilities. Determine actions as you proceed. Be flexible. If necessary, change your focus as you obtain more and better information.

There are various sources of information for you to consult to find out about jobs and job titles in the business world. (See "Employment Resources" in Appendix H and "Sample Career Objectives for Educators" in Appendix C.) You can read the want ad sections of newspapers to find out about and become familiar with job titles and job descriptions. If you decide to answer these newspaper ads, do not become alarmed if you do not receive a reply. The reason for this lack of response is because employers who place these ads receive so many responses that they cannot answer all of them. Therefore, if you do not specifically fit the job description in the ad, you may not want to waste your time answering it.

The yellow pages of the telephone directory may be scanned to identify job categories and potential employers. The white pages of the telephone directory may be consulted under the headings of City and County.

Professional journals and trade magazines often contain want ad sections. Public libraries usually subscribe to these journals and magazines, or you may subscribe on your own whether or not you are a member of the professional organization. An example of a trade magazine is *Publishers Weekly* which lists job openings in the communications and publishing fields.

The business sections of public libraries are invaluable sources of information. They contain directories, handbooks and various information on the labor market. (See "Employment Resources" in Appendix H.) *The Dictionary of Occupational Titles* lists over 20,-000 job titles. You can explain your job search to the librarian and ask for book titles and suggestions to help you in your search.

Another suggestion regarding focusing is to picture yourself in an ideal job and imagine yourself successful in it. Picture yourself looking forward to going to work every day doing something you thoroughly enjoy and which you do well. Keep this in mind while focusing, as it is of utmost importance that you enjoy the job which you will eventually choose.

In focusing, remember that there are line positions and staff positions in a company. The line positions are the decision-making and money-making positions. These are usually better paying and are the ones from which people are promoted to executive positions within the company. Staff positions are support positions and can be subject to lay-off during economic recession. For further information on line and staff positions, refer to the book entitled *Games Mother Never Taught You* (See "Suggested Reading Materials" in Appendix J).

The informational interview (which is discussed in the next chapter) can be used to uncover information about jobs and job titles; however, it is best to have focused upon a particular position before you embark upon an informational interview. People in business have a limited amount of time during the day in which to speak with you, and they can become very uncommunicative if you sit down in front of them and say, "I don't know what I want to do." No one else knows you as well as you know yourself. It is up to you to lay the groundwork and focus upon your own career objective.

Keep faith in yourself as a person with valuable assets, worthwhile accomplishments and professional job skills. Try not to lose sight of these qualities you possess no matter how discouraged you might feel after a bad day. There will be good days and bad days. There will be some days when a great deal of progress will be made and other days when you feel that you haven't made much progress at all. Expect that this will happen.

Recreational outlets are important during this phase of your career search. Have lunch with a friend and discuss ways of improving your methods of focusing. Or, take a walk and try to think through your frustrations. Try to keep a positive attitude devoid of negative thoughts or intrusions. Inner harmony is essential.

You must focus on a career objective before you can interview successfully for information and write a resume. Therefore, this groundwork must be established before proceeding further in your creative job search.

NETWORKING AND INFORMATIONAL INTERVIEWING

Since approximately 80% of all jobs with good salaries and good working conditions are located in what is known as the "hidden job market,"* networking is of utmost importance in any job search. The remaining 20% of all jobs are advertised in newspapers, listed with employment agencies or listed with job recruiters. Most employment agencies list mainly clerical jobs and/or jobs which pay up to $15,000 per year. Also, employment agency fees can be either employee or employer paid.

Answering ads in a newspaper seldom brings any response except for a form letter of rejection. Job recruiters are usually looking only for a person who is already successful in his/her chosen field.

*Richard Irish, *Go Hire Yourself an Employer.* Garden City, New York: Doubleday, 1978, p. 11.

For these reasons, it is important for you to do some networking and informational interviewing.

Networking consists of locating jobs through people you already know. Informational interviewing means exactly what the name implies. It is interviewing another person who has the same type of job in which you might be interested. It is important to interview for information in order to decide whether or not you would like such a job. For instance, if you think you would like to work as a buyer, you can talk with someone who works in that capacity.

You are in control during an informational interview. You can ask about that person's educational background, skills, previous work experience, day-to-day duties, work environment, and other information you feel is pertinent. You can also ask the person for job-hunting ideas and referrals to other people with whom to interview for information. Most people love to talk about their jobs and, since this is not a job interview, it can be a very relaxed situation in an informal setting.

If you don't know the name of anyone in a company with whom to make an appointment for an informational interview, ask friends, relatives and acquaintances for names. There are directories in the business section of the public library, such as *Contacts Influential,* that list the names of people in various positions in companies in metropolitan areas. There may be other employment directories for your area. You may have to ask the reference librarian where these directories are located.

A good way to research companies in order to determine the ones in which you would prefer to work is to consult such sources as *Moody's Industrial Manual, Dun & Bradstreet Million Dollar Directory, Dun & Bradstreet Middle Market Directory, Thomas Register, Standard & Poor's Register, Standard & Poor's Stock Reports,* and *Directory of Corporate Affiliations.* Read the annual reports in order to obtain background information on specific companies. Product knowledge and financial conditions need to be researched thoroughly.

When calling a person to make an appointment for an informational interview, the initial contact may be difficult since you have not met the person at the other end of the telephone line. Make it perfectly clear that you are not looking for a job at this time, but that you are engaged in a career change and are seeking information about a particular job. You might say that you realize the person is not the one who does the hiring, but that you would like to meet with him/her for advice. Or, you might say that you realize there aren't any jobs available, but that you need to consult him/her as an expert in that particular field of specialization. Then, ask for ten minutes of his/her time. If the person tries to interview you over the telephone, say that you would really like to meet him/her in person. Then, ask to set a particular time and date. A good time for an informational interview is toward the end of a person's workday.

Most people will respond in a positive manner to your request for an informational interview if you are sincere. Self-confidence is needed so that your tone of voice reflects an optimistic attitude. With practice, the process of setting up appointments for informational interviews becomes much easier.

In preparing to go on an informational interview, it is a good idea to dress as if you were going on a job interview. First impressions are very important, and you want to make and leave a favorable one. After all, maybe the person with whom you speak will know of a job opening in that company or in another company and will refer you for the job.

Be sure to arrive on time for the informational interview. Also, be sure to carry a list of questions either in your head or written down on paper to ask the person being interviewed.

Do not overstay your welcome when interviewing for information. Play it by ear and when you feel it is time to leave, thank the person and make your exit.

During the informational interview, appear attentive and interested in what the person has to say. Display your best manners and be tactful and courteous. If the person tries to turn the informational interview into a job interview, state that your purpose on that day is to obtain information only. Then, make an appointment for a job interview on a later date.

After you leave the person's office, go somewhere to sit down and evaluate what you have learned. Hopefully, you will have received answers to your questions and further referrals in order to enable you to make an effective career change.

Always follow up an informational interview with a "thank you" letter. The "thank you" letter should be typed on white or off-white paper. It is very important to write a "thank you" letter because it reinforces you in the person's mind. Then, if s/he should hear of a future job opening, you might be referred for the position.

Regarding networking, ask all of your friends, relatives and acquaintances for names, ideas, referrals, and job openings. These people are invaluable contacts in your job search. As more and more people become aware of your job search, the greater your chances become for getting a job suited to your particular talents, interests and abilities.

ORGANIZING YOUR RESUME

In organizing your resume, first remember that business is not interested in educational jargon. Terms which are familiar in the ivory tower are not applicable to the industrial tower. That person behind the desk reading the resumes which pile up every day has but a few seconds to devote to reading about all your hard-earned skills and abilities. The most important thing in this person's mind is your career objective. It must be stated clearly and concisely. You must know this yourself and have the ability to focus on what you want. Your goals must be clear, and your background, education and experience must fit your career objective. Your resume is a short factual statement of who and what you are.

Your resume must be organized, neat, readable, and applicable to the company's needs. If your resume is poorly typed, faintly typed or if there is one misspelled word, it will usually be thrown out immediately.

There are slick resume writers who sell resumes to the gullible job seeker. However, this slick operator does not know you as well as you know yourself, and often this type of resume comes across as "phony" since it is apt to be too smooth and overblown. Thus, it does not reflect the real, unique you. In addition, this type of resume writer is not as familiar with the educational world as you are. He has not been there. You have.

There are different types of formats for resumes. The three most frequently used are:

1. The Chronological format (dates and jobs are listed in order to relate the past to the present)

2. The Informal format (letter form)

3. The Functional format (type of function and level of responsibility are listed)

The functional resume is the type of resume which is recommended for the business world and the type which research has proved to be the most effective in getting job interviews. It includes the following: basic identifying information, career objective, areas of effectiveness, summary of experience, and education. Special talents and skills may be an added heading at the end of the resume.

The functional resume is a summary of your most important skill areas and interests. It uses the action phraseology described in Chapter II. In this type of resume, you can state what your career objective is by listing the type of function and the level of responsibility you are seeking. Under areas of effectiveness, you can highlight work experience areas, self-accomplishment areas and results. Remember to include such things as, "Trained, supervised and evaluated people in individualized tutoring program with 95% success in achieving training objectives." Facts such as this relate to the business world.

Before you start writing your resume, you must list your job skills. For example, if you have analytical and staffing abilities, write them down, using action verbs (refer back to Chapter II and see "Function Words to Describe Skills" in Appendix A.)

Be definitive in writing your resume. List experiences which relate to your career objective. Be realistic, not vague or unrealistic. If you say you want to start as vice president with no experience to back you up, this objective will be so obviously unrealistic that your future employer will be turned off. Also, your future employer does not want to read a list of your skills and abilities in excessive detail with every single thing you have accomplished from nursery school to the present. A resume is not an autobiography!

Incidentally, when sending out your resume, always include a cover letter which serves as an introduction. (Cover letters are discussed in Chapter VII. See "Sample Cover Letter" in Appendix G.) Keep in mind that the reader will want your resume and cover letter to state in simple English your career objective, why you want to work for this particular company, and how you can do the job. Always take the approach, "I am the person best suited for the job, and I fit your particular needs and requirements perfectly." The resume reader is not interested in reading that you are seeking a challenging position in which you desire self-fulfillment. S/he is only interested in the fact that you can do the job.

Remember that you must reschedule your thinking and reprogram yourself from educator to businessman or businesswoman. In order to make yourself saleable to the business community, you must think of your skills and abilities in relation to business. Large businesses receive approximately 1500 to 3500 unsolicited resumes per month. Since the average resume is screened for only *45 seconds,* your resume must be effective. It must stand out from the others. It must make the employer want to talk to you instead of all the other applicants.

Some employers like to see something slightly different, such as paper of fine and unusual quality. But don't go to an extreme. Stay away from bright colors. Your resume should be printed on white or off-white paper. When in doubt, be conservative, as the business world is conservative. Always use good taste.

Do not include a picture of yourself with your resume as this can create a negative effect on a future employer. Do not include personal data which does not relate to the job you are seeking. This unrelated data often confuses the resume reader and causes undue annoyance since this data is not a prerequisite for the job. Do not list references in your resume. If the employer wants them, s/he will request them. Above all, your resume should not be more than one page in length simply because most employers do not have the time to read long resumes. Your 2 or 3 page resume will end up in the wastebasket.

Remember, above all, that your resume must be clear, simply stated and job related. It must be relevant and applicable to the job you are seeking. It must list only one career objective. If you have more than one career objective, the employer will think that you have not focused on a clear goal. You must be definite about what you want and know why you want that particular type of job.

Summary of Rules and Guidelines For Resume Writing

1. Keep the resume clear, specific and relevant to your focus

2. List only one career objective in clear, concise language

3. Avoid redundancy and flowery phrases

4. Avoid educational jargon

5. Focus on your strengths, but do not blow them out of proportion

6. Focus your resume for one employer or one industry

7. Focus on the positive, using strong action verbs in an active, not passive, sense

8. Proofread your resume carefully and check grammar and spelling

9. Use white or off-white paper of good quality

10. Be sure your resume has a clear and readable format with correct margins and headings

11. Avoid all temptations to include irrelevant facts and autobiographical data

12. Keep in mind that your career objective must match all job titles in the areas of effectiveness section (see "Examples of Areas of Effectiveness" in Appendix B)

13. Take your resume to a good printer to be reproduced

14. Remember that your goal is to get an interview and that you must include results (percentages, numbers) along with your job skills

The following books deal with resume writing and may be helpful to you.

Better Job Resumes. New York: Council for Career Planning, 1979.

Bolles, Richard N. *Tea Leaves; A New Look at Resumes.* Berkeley, California: Ten Speed Press, 1978.

Dickhut, Harold W. *Professional Resume: Job Search Guide.* Chicago: Management Counselors, Inc., 1978.

Faux, Marian. *The Complete Resume Guide.* New York: Monarch Press, 1979.

Jameson, Robert J. *Handbook of Outstanding Resumes.* Verona, New Jersey: Performance Dynamics, Inc., 1976.

Koch, Harry W. *Resumes and How to Write Them.* San Francisco: Ken-Books, 1977.

McDaniels, Carl. *Developing A Professional Vita Or Resume.* Garret Park, Maryland: Garret Park Press, 1978.

Specialized Resumes for Executives and Professionals. New York: World Trade Academy Press, 1978.

WRITING YOUR RESUME

You are now ready to write your functional resume. Keep in mind that your resume highlights your experience and skills. It must be neat and orderly, with the sections clearly defined, and one page in length.

Your resume consists of several sections. The basic identifying information, such as your name (in capital letters), address and telephone number (including area code) is located in the first section. Remember that personal information, such as hair color, height, etc., is not included in a resume as it is not pertinent to the job.

The next section of your resume consists of the career objective. Most employers like to see the career objective listed at the top of the resume because it shows that you have thought out what you want to do. An example of a career objective for an educator might be "Manager," "Interpreter" or "Technical Writer." (See "Career Objectives for Educators" in Appendix C.) Your career objective should be clearly stated. It should tell the company what you want rather than what you can offer. You may want to write several resumes each with a different career objective. If you can't write a good career objective, it is better not to write one at all, in which case you can include it in your cover letter instead of stating it on your resume.

Areas of effectiveness would be listed next. (See "Examples of Areas of Effectiveness" in Appendix B.) There should be four areas highlighted in this section. Go back to your skills assessment and choose those skills that you wish to use in your next job. Group them together in terms of similarity. Use only those job skills that are relevant to the position you are seeking. Up to three job titles for each highlighted area may be grouped together and separated by a slash, for example, "Educator/Trainer/Evaluator."

Since a resume is only screened for a few seconds, include only information that is pertinent. You want to immediately impress the person screening your resume with your outstanding qualifications. Always stay away from educational jargon and try to explain your skills in terms of what is of interest to business. For example, state, "Trained staff members," not, "Taught student assistants." Also, keep in mind that business is interested in results. After, "Trained staff members," you might add, "Achieved success in 8 out of 10 cases."

The fourth section of your functional resume consists of a summary of your work experience listed in chronological order with the most recent work experience listed first. Thoroughly annotate your experience. Instead of listing items by actual job title, try to list them according to the tasks performed. For example, instead of listing "Teacher" use a word such as "Instructor," "Educator," "Cross-Cultural Relations Specialist," etc. Dates need not be listed on your resume.

Education usually is best listed in the last section of your functional resume in chronological order with your most recent degree listed first.

If you wish to highlight special skills and abilities which are pertinent to the job you are seeking, these are listed after the education section.

Now, you need only to refine and review your resume before it can be printed for distribution.

WRITING A COVER LETTER FOR YOUR RESUME

When sending your resume to a prospective employer, always include a cover letter geared as closely as possible to the specific job for which you are applying. You should use similar phrases and terms as those used in the job description, as well as emphasize the fact that your career objective and job skills match the employer's needs. (A sample cover letter is located in Appendix G.)

The cover letter should be stimulating, coherent, interesting, and should be addressed to a specific person in the company. If you do not know whom to send it to, check in the business section of the local public library in directories, such as *Contacts Influential,* that list the names of people in various positions in companies. Check for any other employment directories for your area. (You may want to ask the reference librarian for assistance.)

36

Your most recent job experience outlining your position and duties should be explained in the cover letter. Stay away from educational phraseology. Use language that is relevant to the business world. If possible, mention what you can do differently from others and give the impression that you would be an asset to the company.

Never state in your cover letter that you wish to use your skills and abilities to the greatest potential. The company is only interested in its own needs and how you can fulfill them. State clearly that you can do . . . . for them to meet . . . . needs. Always think in terms of what they want and how you can match their requirements to mutual advantage.

In the last paragraph of the cover letter, either specify a particular date that you will call for an interview or ask, "May I hear from you?" Remember that the cover letter is selling you! Its purpose and the purpose of the resume are to get an interview so that you can sell yourself and get the job.

INTERVIEWING FOR THE JOB

The job interview is crucial. It is the goal for which you have so carefully prepared yourself in your job search thus far. You must be prepared to handle it with grace, dignity, self-confidence, and poise. To accomplish the best results, you should first know why you want the job and second know why you are well suited and well qualified for that particular job.

The interview is a stress situation. You must be sure of yourself. If you hesitate or show any indication of lack of self-confidence, you create a negative, unfavorable image.

The following is a list of questions frequently asked by interviewers during job interviews. Look over the list, prepare and memorize strong answers to each of these questions so that you will not be caught off guard. Then, practice interviewing with a close friend and get feedback on your answers. Hopefully, your answers will indicate that you feel good about yourself. Your answers must be memorized so that you do not show any signs of nervousness or inability to react favorably under stress. During the interview, listen carefully and attentively to the interviewer in order to control the situation and get a feel for his/her style and value judgments. You must be able to perceive from the interviewer's words and phrases what s/he wants to hear in the way of a response to a question so that you can answer it to your best advantage. When answering a question, try to use the same words and phrases as used by the interviewer.

Questions Frequently Asked During Job Interviews

Tell me about yourself.

Are you interested in a job or a career? Why?

What are your strong points? Weak points?

What are your most outstanding contributions and achievements?

How do you react under stress and pressure?

Are you self-motivated? Organized? Give examples.

What are your future career plans?

What three adjectives would you use to describe yourself?

Where do you see yourself 5 years from now? Where do you see yourself 10 years from now? What position do you see yourself holding in 5 or 10 years?

How do you occupy yourself in your leisure time?

Explain how you would handle supervisory responsibilities in a situation of employee unrest?

What do you know about our company and why do you want to work for our firm?

Why did you choose this particular field of work?

What is your ultimate career goal? Why did you choose this goal?

Why should we hire you?

Have you ever been dismissed from a previous job? For what reason?

Why are you leaving (did you leave) your last job?

How did you relate to your previous employer? Were you treated well by him or her?

What is your experience in supervising others?

If hired, how long do you plan to stay in this job?

What two or three things are most important to you in your job?

What is your salary range? What is the least salary you would accept? How much do you expect to be earning in 10 years?

Why are you changing careers?

What can I do for you?

What are your long-term goals? Short-term goals?

Have you ever been unemployed? For how long?

If you were financially independent, what would you do with your time?

Why did you apply for this particular position?

What job would you like if you were starting over again in your career?

What things did you like best about your former position?

What things did you like least about your former position?

What was wrong with your last job?

Do you get along with people?

What is your strongest qualification for this job?

What job are you seeking in the next few years?

Have you ever thought about going into business for yourself?

How do you see yourself fitting into our organization?

Why have you held so many jobs?

How did you decide upon your career?

Why do you want to leave your present position at this time?

Have you told your present employer that you are planning to leave?

What interests you most about this job?

Have you developed any new goals lately? If so, what are they?

What interests you most about our methods of production?

Are you more comfortable working with other people or by yourself?

What would you do if there were a conflict in the company between . . . . and . . . . ?

Do you have any plans for furthering your education?

Have you initiated a creative innovation? If so, tell me about it.

Do you analyze well? Give an example of effective analysis of a problem you have solved.

Remember that many of the above-listed questions are a test to see how well you communicate and how spontaneously you can think. The interviewer is usually not looking for a specific answer. He is rating you on how you meet the challenge of his inquiries.

In addition, remember that the interviewer will want to hire you only if you meet the following three conditions: 1. You must have something positive to offer his/her organization, 2. S/he believes your qualifications fit the company's needs, and 3. S/he likes you.

When faced with stress-situation questions, it is human nature to freeze, panic or develop a sick feeling in the pit of your stomach. No one is perfectly prepared. It is therefore permissible to pause before answering a question. If you are asked a question such as, "What would you do if . . . . ," it is advisable to reply, "I would like to think it over for a few minutes," or, "I would consider doing . . . . ," rather than offering an immediate solution. You do not want to commit yourself to one pat answer in case the employer disagrees with your solution to the problem.

You must figure out your own answers to the questions most frequently asked during interviews. In answering, try to address the concern rather than the question. Always concentrate on guessing what the major concern behind the question might be so that your answer can target in on this concern.

The following suggestions may be helpful in formulating ideas for answers to some of the stress questions.

Q. "Why are you changing careers?"

A. "I am not changing careers; I am using my same skills in a different way." (This answer avoids the trap of a forced entry level position.)

Q. "What is your ultimate professional goal?"

A. "That's really tough. Let me think about it for a few seconds."

Q. "What do you see yourself doing in 5 or 10 years?"

A. "I hope that in 5 or 10 years I will have advanced as far as my capabilities will take me."

Q. "Do you think a woman could handle this job as well as a man?"

A. "Perhaps you could explain to me the requirements of the job which are different for a woman than for a man." (Do not show annoyance.)

Q. "How did your previous employer treat you?"

A. "My previous employer showed confidence in my ability to do a good job by always treating me with respect and courtesy." (Never make the slightest derogatory remark about a previous employer as this could backfire against you.)

Q. "What are your strengths?"

A. "My strengths are in the areas of effective communication, supervision, and organization."

Q. "What are your weaknesses?"

A. "A weakness of mine is that I expect as much from subordinates as from myself. Since I am a hard worker, I expect the same high standard of performance from those who are assisting me." (Turn a weakness into a strength.)

One final word of advice is to be sure that you do not appear too glib with the answers that you have prepared in advance for the stress questions. It is tempting to become overcasual and assume an informal, flippant pose. This is seldom appreciated by a prospective employer. Employers usually do not hire overbearing, overaggressive, conceited, know-it-all people!

Overall, job interviews are subjective. There is not a perfect answer which will guarantee 100 percent success in getting a job offer. Since you will usually have to undergo several interviews before a position is offered, you will want to display behavior which creates a positive impression and results in an invitation to return for a second interview.

It is illegal for the interviewer to ask certain questions about family obligations, personal data and job requirements during a job interview. These include the following:

How old are you?

Do you plan to get married?

Do you plan to have children?

Do you have children? If so, how many and what are their ages? (This may have to be reported after employment for insurance purposes.)

How long have you resided at your present address?

Have you ever had your wages garnished?

Have you ever been convicted of a felony or a misdemeanor? (Federal Courts have held that a conviction for a felony or misdemeanor may not by itself lawfully constitute an absolute bar to employment, but that an employer may give fair consideration to the relationship between a conviction and the applicant's fitness for a particular job. These decisions indicate that conviction records should be cause for rejection only if their number, nature and recentness would cause the applicant to be unsuitable for the position. If such inquiries are made, they should be accompanied by a statement that a conviction record will not necessarily be a bar to employment, and that factors such as age and time of the offense, seriousness and nature of the violation, and rehabilitation will be taken into account.)

Have you ever been discharged from military service?

Have you ever filed bankruptcy?

Do you own your house?

Do you rent your house?

Do you own your car?

What is your religion?

What is your racial ethnic group?

Are you available for work on weekends and holidays? (If such a question is asked, it must be asked of both men and women, and employer must respect employee's religious needs and beliefs.)

Are you a citizen of the United States?

How will you handle the care of your children while you're working?

Are you free to travel? (This question may be asked if it is an occupational qualification.)

How does your husband/wife feel about traveling or working overtime?

The last three questions may be asked during a job interview only if they are directed at both men and women. If they are asked only of women or only of men, they are illegal questions.

The above list of illegal questions has been formulated according to the latest government publications regarding fair pre-employment inquiries versus unfair pre-employment inquiries. The law at present, interpreted through court rulings and EEOC (Equal Employment Opportunity Commission) decisions, prohibits the use of all pre-employment inquiries and qualifying factors which disproportionately screen out members of minority groups or members of one sex and are not valid predictors of successful job performance or cannot be justified by "business necessity."

For further information on court and EEOC decisions, contact: Educational Programs Branch, U.S. Equal Opportunity Commission, 2401 E Street, N.W., Room 4295, Washington, D.C. 20506. For further information on age discrimination, contact: Employment Standards Administration, Wage and Hour Division, U.S. Department of Labor, Washington, D.C. 20310.

Individual states have their own rules regarding Fair Employment Practices and Labor Standards Enforcement. These divisions are part of the Industrial Relations Department within each state. Inquiries may be made to the Fair Employment Practices Office in your state. Publications are usually available and mailed to you free of charge upon request.

If you are asked an illegal question, you can do one of two things. You can refuse to answer it on the grounds that it is an illegal question (in which case the interviewer may label you as a troublemaker) or you can ask politely how that particular question is related to the job.

During the interview, your answers to questions which may be rated as positive or negative concern such things as maturity level, emotional stability, even temper, team cooperation, tact, adaptability, aggressiveness, self-assertiveness, self-discipline, initiative, follow-through, self-confidence, conscientiousness, judgment, reliability, honesty, sincerity, working efficiency, etc. These things are often reflections of character traits which the interviewer may decide as a plus or minus depending on how you react and respond to him/her. Your attitude and body language reveal a great deal. For example, you should project a responsible attitude by accepting and learning from your own limitations and failures rather than project an irresponsible attitude by rationalizing failures and limitations.

PERTINENT INFORMATION FOR INTERVIEWING

Promptness. Be on time. Arrive at least five minutes before the scheduled time of the interview. (Allow for traffic congestion, etc.) Do not bring a friend.

Appearance. Be neat, clean and well-groomed. Wear a business suit with matching coat/skirt (women) and coat/pants (men) in conservative colors (black, navy blue).

Nervousness. Do not display outward signs of nervousness, such as fiddling with glasses or other objects. Keep your hands folded in your lap. Establish eye contact and maintain good posture. Keep voice steady.

Greeting. Greet the interviewer by name. Take cues from interviewer on whether or not to shake hands and where to sit. If interviewer shakes your hand, use a firm grip. Wait to be asked to be seated. Do not chew gum. Do not smoke unless invited to do so.

Preparation. Expect stress questions and personal questions. (This is where it is important to have prepared answers in advance.) Do not display emotions, such as anger, surprise or fear.

Salesmanship and Self-Promotion. Sell yourself. Stick to job-related points that will reveal your skills, aptitudes, interests, strengths, and efficient work habits.

Clarity. Be clear about your career objective. Do not say that you will do "anything."

Application Form. Try to avoid filling out an application form, if possible, as most of the better-paying jobs do not require one. If you must fill one out, do so as neatly and completely as possible. (A sloppy application form leaves the impression of a sloppy worker.)

Salary. If you are asked what minimum salary you will accept, state firmly that you never discuss salary until a definite job offer has been made. If asked what your present salary is, you can either tell the truth or withhold the information until later.

Honesty. If asked why you left teaching, tell the truth in terms that business will be able to understand. If your job has been terminated due to lack of sufficient funds for public education, state it without bitterness or wrath against the school system. If your field has been eliminated from the curriculum, this is a justifiable reason for leaving the educational field. State this in terms which are clear and concise and without embellishment. Never dwell on your rotten breaks or make any slighting, damaging, remarks about your former employer.

The following are questions that you should ask a prospective employer during a job interview. It is important for you to find out everything you possibly can in order to make a decision as to whether or not you would like to work for that particular company. You will want to ask intelligent questions in order to reveal your degree of interest in the company and serve to impress the interviewer with your degree and level of intelligence. Careful timing of these questions should be considered. A "1" indicates that the question should be asked during the initial interview. A "2" indicates that the question should be asked during subsequent interview(s).

Questions to Ask the Interviewer

(1) What are the three main areas of responsibility of the position? (Exactly what will be my duties?)

(1) What will be expected of me in this job? Is there a written job description?

(1) What kind of training will I receive? From whom? For how long?

(1) What criteria will be used to evaluate me and who will be the evaluator? Does this lead to promotion? If so, when?

(1) What things about the organization and structure of the company do I need to know which are relevant to my position?

(1) Who will be my immediate boss? Will I report to him/her or to someone else? Where will I fit into the organization?

(1) What do you, the interviewer, like best about this organization/structure?

(1 or 2) What about the future? What are the possibilities for advancement?

(2) How many people have held this job during the last five years?

(2) Are job listings posted for upward or lateral movement within the company?

(2) What has happened to the last two or three people who held this job? Have they been promoted? If so, to what position?

(2) How often can I expect an evaluation of job performance and is there a salary increase at this time? (Salary increases are often based on performance or merit and occur every 3 to 18 months, depending upon company policy.)

(2) What is the salary range for my particular job classification? What are the entry level, mid-level and maximum salary levels? (Mid-level is usually a control point.)

(2) What will my working environment be like? Will I be working alone or with others? How many will share the office? If I'm working with others, how many are on a team? Will the working area be noisy or quiet? How many interruptions can I expect?

(2) What are the extra job compensations and fringe benefits, such as overtime pay, bonuses, disability insurance, life insurance, medical insurance, dental insurance, pension plans, credit unions, stock and investment opportunities, profit-sharing plans, etc. If a profit-sharing plan is offered, what percentage is contributed by the company and how long must I be employed before it takes effect? (This can vary from several months to several years.) Also, is my date of eligibility from January 1 or from the date I begin employment with the company?

(2) Are there compensations for travel? Company car? Insurance? Expense account?

(2) May I see my work location?

(2) What about the work schedule? Are there shifts? When does the work day begin? End? Is there a four-day work week with ten hour days? Is the work week flexible? Will there be work to take home? Will there be evening or weekend business duties? How often? Where?

(2) What about job-related expenses? Will I have to pay for them? Car? Mileage? Insurance?

(2) What about moving expenses?

(2) Is there sick leave pay? For many days per year?

(2) What are the possibilities for expanding my duties in order to create a more responsible position for future opportunity and advancement? If duties are expanded and job title is changed, what is the possi-

bility of a higher salary to match my skills and added responsibility?

If you are offered a job at the end of the interview, never accept or reject it at that time. Instead, ask if you can have a few days to think it over. After the interviewer and you have decided upon a mutual date for your response, assure him/her that you will contact him/her on that date.

If you decide to accept the job, ask for a firm commitment in a letter of employment or contract stating job title, salary and other terms of employment. Since most managers in top positions hate to be held accountable for anything on which they put their names, you may get a bare-bones letter. If you receive such a response, you might wish to write two letters. Write the first letter to the person who interviewed and hired you. This is a response to his/her letter of employment or contract. State that you are delighted to begin working for . . . . on . . . . date, that you think your salary of . . . . is fair and that you are looking forward to semi-annual (or other) reviews of your work, and that you understand that your evaluation will be based on your performance in a job described to you as . . . and . . ., and . . . . State that you are looking forward to joining the profit sharing plan on . . . . date and that you are pleased that your vacation will be . . . . weeks with long weekends and holidays on . . . . dates.

Write the second letter to the president of the company or to the division manager. State that you have accepted the position of . . . . at . . . . salary and that you understand that there will be an evaluation of your job performance in . . . . months. Mention that . . . . hired you and that you are looking forward to working with him/her. State the terms you have agreed upon with the person who hired you.

Keep a copy of the letter of employment or contract and copies of each of the two letters you write. Employers often forget the details of job negotiations and this will be insurance against future misunderstandings.

Always remember to thank the interviewer for the time s/he has spent with you. Thank him/her in person and again by writing a thank you letter after you have left the interview. Remember to express courtesy and sincere gratitude. This is important in order to reinforce yourself in the interviewer's mind and is especially important in case someone else is offered the job and for some reason declines to accept it. In this case, the person most likely to be considered next for the job is the person who has taken the time and trouble to thank the interviewer by letter and point out his/her good qualities (for example, patience, sensitivity, professional manner, etc.)

If you are unsuccessful during an interview, remember to learn from it and go on to the next one with more self-confidence. Do not give up, as there is a job somewhere for you. Keep on trying. Persistence, patience and perseverance are needed.

If the job is not offered to you and if you are brave and willing to accept constructive criticism and to take a risk, call the interviewer and ask whether s/he would be willing to share with you the things which kept you from getting the job. Assure him/her that this information would help you a great deal in learning how to strengthen yourself. Then, use this information to your advantage in your next job interview.

Display a self-confident attitude and manner during your creative job search. If you work at it long enough, you are bound to find the job you want. Good luck!

APPENDIX A

Function Words to Describe Skills

ACCOMPLISH	CREATE	INDEX	PROMOTE
ACHIEVE	DECIDE	INFLUENCE	PROPOSE
ACT	DEFINE	INFORM	PROVIDE
ADAPT	DELEGATE	INITIATE	PUBLICIZE
ADJUST	DEMONSTRATE	INNOVATE	PUBLISH
ADMINISTER	DESIGN	INSPECT	RECOMMEND
ADVERTISE	DETAIL	INSTALL	RECONCILE
ADVISE	DETERMINE	INSTITUTE	RECORD
AFFECT	DEVELOP	INSTRUCT	RECRUIT
ANALYZE	DEVISE	INTEGRATE	RECTIFY
ANTICIPATE	DIRECT	INTERPRET	RE-DESIGN
APPLY	DISTRIBUTE	INTERVIEW	RELATE
APPROACH	DRAFT	INVESTIGATE	RENEW
APPROVE	EDIT	INVENT	REPORT
ARRANGE	EDUCATE	LEAD	REPRESENT
ASSEMBLE	ENCOURAGE	MAINTAIN	RESEARCH
ASSESS	ENLARGE	MANAGE	RESOLVE
ASSIGN	ENLIST	MANIPULATE	REVIEW
ASSIST	ESTABLISH	MARKET	REVISE
ATTAIN	ESTIMATE	MEDIATE	SCAN
AUTHOR	EVALUATE	MERCHANDISE	SCHEDULE
BUDGET	EXAMINE	MODERATE	SCREEN
BUILD	EXCHANGE	MODIFY	SELECT
CALCULATE	EXECUTE	MONITOR	SERVE
CATALOG	EXPAND	MOTIVATE	SPEAK
CHAIR	EXPEDITE	NEGOTIATE	STAFF
CLARIFY	FACILITATE	OBTAIN	STANDARDIZE
COLLABORATE	FAMILIARIZE	OPERATE	STIMULATE
COMMUNICATE	FORECAST	ORGANIZE	SUMMARIZE
COMPARE	FORMULATE	ORIGINATE	SUPERVISE
CONCEIVE	FUND RAISE	PARTICIPATE	SURVEY
CONCEPTUALIZE	GENERATE	PERCEIVE	SYNTHESIZE
CONCILIATE	GOVERN	PERFORM	SYSTEMATIZE
CONDUCT	GUIDE	PERSUADE	TEACH
CONSULT	HANDLE	PLAN	TEAM BUILD
CONTRACT	HIRE	PRESENT	TRAIN
CONTROL	IDENTIFY	PRESIDE	TRANSMIT
COOPERATE	IMPLEMENT	PROBLEM SOLVE	UPDATE
COORDINATE	IMPROVE	PROCESS	UTILIZE
COUNSEL	INCREASE	PRODUCE	WRITE

APPENDIX B

Examples Of Areas Of Effectiveness

ADMINISTRATOR

ANALYST

ANALYZER

ARTIST

COMMUNICATOR

COMMUNITY ORGANIZER

COMMUNITY RELATIONS EXPERT

COORDINATOR

CONSULTANT

COUNSELOR

CROSS-CULTURAL RELATIONS SPECIALIST

DEFINER

DESIGNER

DEVELOPER

DIRECTOR

EDITOR

EDUCATOR

EVALUATOR

FUND RAISER

FINANCIAL RESEARCHER/ PLANNER/ANALYST

FORECASTER

GROUP LEADER

GROUP FACILITATOR

INTERPRETER

INTERVIEWER

LIAISON

MANAGER

MARKETING SPECIALIST

MEDIA SPECIALIST

MEDIATOR

NEGOTIATOR

OPERATIONS ANALYST

ORGANIZATION ANALYST

ORGANIZER

PERSONNEL SPECIALIST

PERSUADER

PLANNER

PRODUCER

PROGRAM DESIGNER

PROGRAM DEVELOPER

PROGRAM ANALYST

PROMOTER

PUBLIC RELATIONS EXPERT

REPORTER

RESEARCHER

RESEARCH ANALYST

SALES

SUPERVISOR

SYSTEMS ANALYST

SYSTEMS DESIGNER

SYSTEMS EXPERT

THERAPIST

TRAINER

WRITER

Reproduced by permission of Ranny Riley & Assoc.©

APPENDIX C

Sample Career Objectives For Educators

ADMINISTRATOR

AGRICULTURAL
MARKETING
SPECIALIST

ARTIST

BUDGET MANAGER

BUYER

COMMUNICATIONS
SPECIALIST

COMMUNITY
RELATIONS
SPECIALIST

COMPENSATION
ANALYST

COMPUTER
PROGRAMMER

COPY WRITER

CROSS CULTURAL
RELATIONS
SPECIALIST

DESIGNER

ECONOMIC
ANALYST

EDITOR

FASHION DESIGNER

HUMAN RELATIONS
SPECIALIST

HUMAN RESOURCES
SPECIALIST

ILLUSTRATOR

INTERIOR
DECORATOR

INTERPRETER

LAB SUPERVISOR

LABOR RELATIONS
SPECIALIST

MANAGER

MARKETING
SPECIALIST

MEDIA SPECIALIST

PERSONNEL
ADMINISTRATOR

PERSONNEL
SPECIALIST

PRODUCTION
SUPERVISOR

PUBLIC
INFORMATION
SPECIALIST

PUBLIC RELATIONS
SPECIALIST

RESEARCH
ANALYST

SALES

SALES PROMOTER

SUPERVISOR

SYSTEMS ANALYST

TECHNICAL WRITER

TRAINING
SPECIALIST

VOCATIONAL
REHABILITATION
SPECIALIST

WRITER

APPENDIX D

Sample Functional Resume For a Teacher

JOHN M. JONES 156 Pine Street Telephone
Burlingame, California 94010 (415) 555-8890

CAREER OBJECTIVE Writer for journals and/or magazines.

AREAS OF EFFECTIVENESS

WRITER/EDITOR Conceived, wrote and sold own poetry and prose for academic journals and other publications. Organized, supervised and edited monthly news publication with a circulation of 5,000.

Edited and planned publication layouts for professional association. Edited, wrote and coordinated special report for State Accreditation Committee.

Wrote and published articles on successful methods of motivating people toward self-actualization.

COMMUNICATOR Communicated effectively with people of diverse ages, backgrounds and skills.

Negotiated agreements and contracts with publishers.

Developed and marketed individualized audio-visual instructional materials.

Planned, organized and coordinated model English studies program for two years.

RESEARCHER Researched, designed and wrote innovative programs involving teamwork for 350 people.

Researched and wrote pertinent biographical data for community library for permanent public display.

Researched and wrote proposals for federal funding of innovative English course.

SUPERVISOR Trained, supervised and evaluated people in individualized tutoring program with 95% success in achieving training objectives. Interviewed, selected, supervised, and evaluated department personnel.

Solved human relations problems among co-workers, administrators and subordinates.

Developed, analyzed and evaluated department goals and objectives.

SUMMARY OF EXPERIENCE

Coordinator/Instructor, High School, San Francisco, Ca.
Instructor, High School, San Jose, Ca.

EDUCATION M.A.: English, University of California, Berkeley, Ca.
B.A.: English, University of California, Davis, Ca.

59

APPENDIX E

Sample Functional Resume For a Counselor

SALLY M. JOHNSON   925 Oak Street   Telephone
                            Santa Clara, California 95154   (408) 555-8903

CAREER OBJECTIVE   Personnel Administrator

AREAS OF EFFECTIVENESS

ADMINISTRATOR

Planned, organized and directed vocational counseling program affecting staff of 10.

Organized and conducted training workshops for 40 people.

Diagnosed and analyzed department's problems with 95% effectiveness in solution of problems.

**COUNSELOR/
INTERVIEWER**

Interviewed and recruited applicants for position openings.

Interviewed, tested and registered applicants from diverse national and international backgrounds for admission to educational institution.

Counseled applicants regarding college entrance requirements and application policies and procedures.

Counseled early-terminating personnel concerning job stress and re-entry anxiety.

Guided people in making suitable career decisions.

**ORGANIZER/
COORDINATOR**

Organized and established schedules for 500 people.

Coordinated educational institution/community project involving 20 people with favorable results.

Organized on-the-job training programs, achieving success in 9 out of 10 cases.

**PUBLIC RELATIONS
SPECIALIST**

Developed cooperative public relations program between educational institution and community.

Served on various community projects, including Mayor's Forum on Career Development.

Persuaded management team and Board of Trustees to adopt vocational education program.

SUMMARY OF EXPERIENCE

Vocational Guidance Counselor, Knox College, San Jose, Ca.
Coordinator/Counselor, High School, Sunnyvale, Ca.
Instructor, High School, Santa Cruz, Ca.

EDUCATION

M.S.: Guidance and Counseling, Mills College, Oakland, Ca.
B.A.: English, University of the Pacific, Stockton, Ca.

APPENDIX F

Sample Functional Resume For a Librarian

ROBERT A. NELSON   1927 Main Street   Telephone
                      San Francisco, California 94404   (415) 555-0098

CAREER OBJECTIVE   Manager

AREAS OF EFFECTIVENESS

MANAGER

Managed and administered entire library operation, including purchasing, budgeting, goal setting, program development.

Budgeted and allocated funds for books, materials, supplies, equipment.

Developed, coordinated and integrated library goals and objectives to meet goals, objectives, standards, and requirements of 12 other departments.

Supervised professional and clerical staff of 10.

MEDIA SPECIALIST

Developed and maintained large audio-visual collection for people of diverse ages, backgrounds and skills.

Instructed personnel in use of audio-visual materials and equipment.

Planned, organized and produced audio-visual materials for use in job training programs.

TRAINER

Developed training programs for 10 staff members with 98% effectiveness in achieving training objectives.

Selected and trained 10 staff members for research project.

Developed, organized and coordinated volunteer program. Trained volunteers on major project.

ORGANIZER/ COORDINATOR

Organized community participation to facilitate installation of detection system to reduce book losses.

Surveyed, analyzed and coordinated budget projections for entire institution.

Surveyed library population in order to tabulate results of library usage for future planning.

SUMMARY OF EXPERIENCE

Coordinator/Director, High School Media Center, San Jose, Ca.
Media Specialist, Jr. High School, San Rafael, Ca.
Instructor, High School, South San Francisco, Ca.

EDUCATION

M.A.: Library Science, Tulane University, New Orleans, La.
B.A.: English, University of California, Berkeley, Ca.

63

APPENDIX G

Sample Cover Letter

3534 Main Street
Burlingame, California
94010
April 15, 19

Mr. John Smith, Manager
Smith and Company
191 South C Street
San Mateo, California 94401

Dear Mr. Smith:

It has been brought to my attention that you are in the process of expanding your Public Relations Division. Since research has indicated that your firm is growing and progressive, I would like to work for you.

In my present and previous positions, I have accumulated several years of experience in public relations work. You will note from my resume that some of my accomplishments include organizing and publicizing a scholarship fund, editing and publishing a monthly newspaper with a circulation of 2,400, writing goals, objectives and job descriptions for department members, and writing a brochure integrating these department goals and objectives with those of other departments.

My education includes a bachelor's degree from Pomona College, several credits toward a master's degree, plus several credits in computer science. Since my educational background and experience are supportive of my career goal as a Public Relations Specialist, I feel that I would be an asset to Smith and Company.

I will call you on Wednesday, April 20, to arrange for a personal interview.

Yours truly,

Sara Thompson

APPENDIX H

Employment Resources
(Some Sources of Information For Job Seekers)

1. Informational Interviews and Networking (see Chapter IV).

2. News Media (such as newspapers, radio, television, news magazines).
   Note stories which indicate that new jobs will be opening, such as "ABC Company will be opening a new plant next year" or "XYZ Company will be expanding its facilities to include . . . . "

3. Yellow Pages of Telephone Directory.
   Check the category "Associations."

4. Professional Journals, Newsletters and Magazines.
   Get these from friends, the library, or subscribe on your own. Research the want ads in these publications. Example: *Publishers Weekly*—job openings in the communications field are listed.

5. Company Newsletters.
   Discover openings before they are published.

6. Libraries.
   Check to see if the public library has resource materials helpful to the job seeker. Consult the librarian for help.

7. Directories.
   Research directories in the business section of the public library. Ask the reference librarian where they are located.
   Examples: *Contacts Influential*—business executives according to company and title are listed by personal names.
   Directory of Directories—names and addresses of directories are listed.
   Directory of National Trade and Professional Associations
   Dun & Bradstreet, Inc.—large corporations are listed.
   Encyclopedia of Associations—approximately 500 professional associations are listed.
   The Foundation Directory—organizations which give grants are listed.
   Standard Rate and Data—publications in every field are listed.

8. Unions.
   Contact union officials to find out if they have job placement services.

9. Special Interest Groups.
   Contact the one(s) which you think might be of help to you.
   Examples: Chamber of Commerce (weekly job forums in which panels of business people give advice to job seekers in some cities)

College Alumnae Offices
Rotary, Lions, Kiwanis Clubs
Veterans Administration
Women's Centers
Women's Professional Organizations
Men's Professional Organizations

10. State Employment Agencies.
    Take advantage of such services as employment counseling, employment
    opportunities and listings.

11. City and County Personnel Offices.
    Get list of current job openings.

12. U.S. Civil Service Commission.
    Consult job information centers in large cities for job listings. (Tests are required
    for employment with the federal government.)

13. Private Employment Agencies.
    Check for job opportunity listings with one that handles your area of interest.
    (Beware of possible fees—either employer paid or employee paid.) (Most jobs are
    clerical in nature and pay only up to $15,000 per year.)

14. Want Ads.
    Scan want ads in Sunday editions of newspapers as they usually contain a greater
    number of listings than daily papers. (Unfortunately, only about 15% of all jobs
    are obtained through want ads.)

15. Placement Offices (colleges, universities).
    Check for job opening referrals. (Usually for graduates only.)

16. Career Guides.
    Consult various employer and executive recruiter directories for your area.

APPENDIX J

Suggested Reading Materials

Albee, Lou. *Job Hunting After Forty.* New York: Arc Books, 1972.

Bolles, Richard N. *The Quick Job Hunting Map.* Berkeley, California: Ten Speed Press, 1977.

———. *Tea Leaves; A New Look at Resumes.* Berkeley, California: Ten Speed Press, 1976.

———. *The Three Boxes of Life.* Berkeley, California: Ten Speed Press, 1978.

———. *What Color Is Your Parachute?* Berkeley, California: Ten Speed Press, 1978.

Crystal, John C. and Richard N. Bolles. *Where Do I Go from Here with My Life: A Workbook for Career-Seekers and Career Changers.* Berkeley, California: Ten Speed Press, 1974.

Djeddah, Eli. *Moving Up.* Berkeley, California: Ten Speed Press, 1978.

———. *Now That I Know Which Side Is Up.* Berkeley, California: Ten Speed Press, 1976.

Harragan, Betty L. *Games Mother Never Taught You; Corporate Gamemanship for Women.* New York: Rawson, 1977.

Hennig, Margaret and Anne Jardim. *The Managerial Woman.* Garden City, New York: Doubleday, 1977.

Holland, John L. *Making Vocational Choices; A Theory of Careers.* Englewood Cliffs, New Jersey: Prentice-Hall, 1973.

Irish, Richard K. *Go Hire Yourself an Employer.* Garden City, New York: Doubleday, 1978.

Jackson, Tom and Davidyne Mayleas. *The Hidden Job Market; A System to Beat the System.* New York: Times Books, 1976.

Lakein, Alan. *How to Get Control of Your Time and Your Life.* New York: McKay, 1973.

Molloy, John T. *Dress for Success.* New York: McKay, 1975.

———. *The Woman's Dress for Success Book.* Chicago: Follett, 1977.

Williams, Marcille Gray. *The New Executive Woman: A Guide to Business Success.* New York: Chilton, 1977.

Wortman, Max S., Jr. and JoAnn Sperling. *Defining the Manager's Job.* New York: American Management Association, 1975.

INDEX